BOOK TWO

A DOZEN A DAY
SONGBOOK

Easy Classical

Including music from Bach, Chopin, Fauré,
Handel, Massenet, Vivaldi plus many more...

T0078997

Arrangements, engravings and audio supplied by Camden Music Services.
CD audio arranged, programmed and mixed by Jeremy Birchall and Christopher Hussey.
Edited by Sam Lung.
CD recorded, mixed and mastered by Jonas Persson.

Printed in the EU.

Order No. WMR101266
ISBN: 978-1-78038-912-7

WILLIS MUSIC

EXCLUSIVELY DISTRIBUTED BY

Visit Hal Leonard Online at
www.halleonard.com

Contact us:
Hal Leonard
7777 West Bluemound Road
Milwaukee, WI 53213
Email: info@halleonard.com

In Europe, contact:
Hal Leonard Europe Limited
42 Wigmore Street
Marylebone, London, W1U 2RY
Email: info@halleonardeurope.com

In Australia, contact:
Hal Leonard Australia Pty. Ltd.
4 Lentara Court
Cheltenham, Victoria, 3192 Australia
Email: info@halleonard.com.au

This collection of well-known classical pieces can be used on its own or as supplementary material to the iconic *A Dozen A Day* techniques series by Edna Mae Burnam. The pieces have been arranged to progress gradually, applying concepts and patterns from Burnam's technical exercises whenever possible. Suggested guidelines for use with the original series are also provided.

These arrangements are excellent supplements for any method and may also be used for sight-reading practice for more advanced students.

The difficulty titles of certain editions of the *A Dozen A Day* books may vary internationally. This repertoire book corresponds to the third difficulty level.

Contents

Each track is split—hear both piano and accompaniment if the balance is centred, and the accompaniment only if the balance control is to the right!

Nimrod
from 'ENIGMA' VARIATIONS

Use with A Dozen A Day Book Two, after Group I (page 4)

Composed by Sir Edward Elgar
Arranged by Christopher Hussey

TRACKS
1–2

Adagio

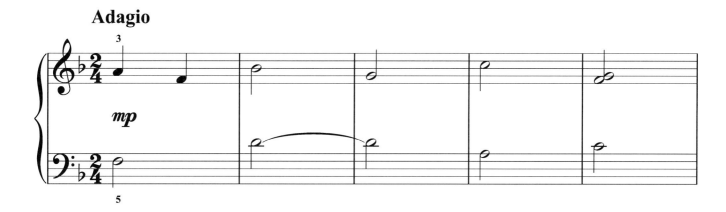

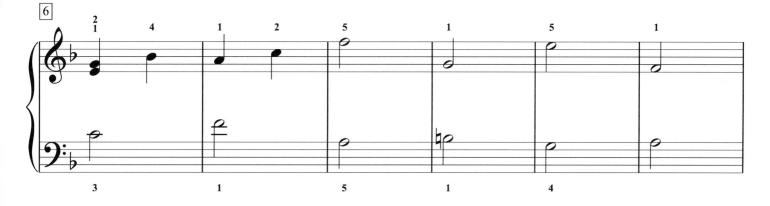

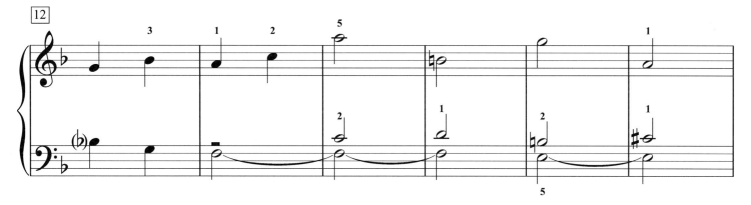

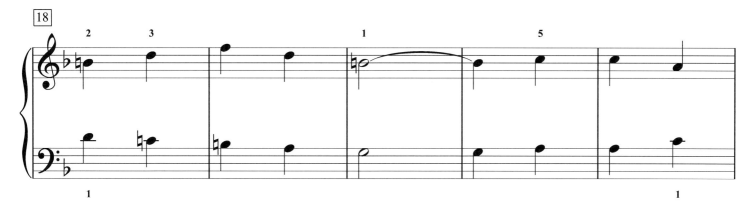

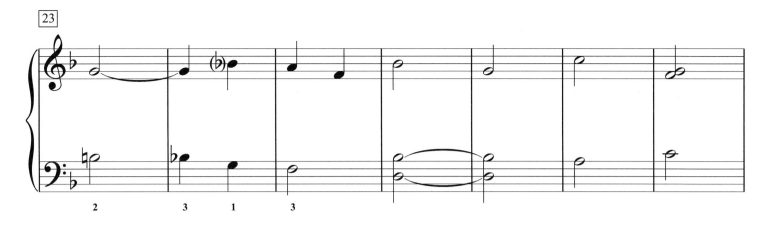

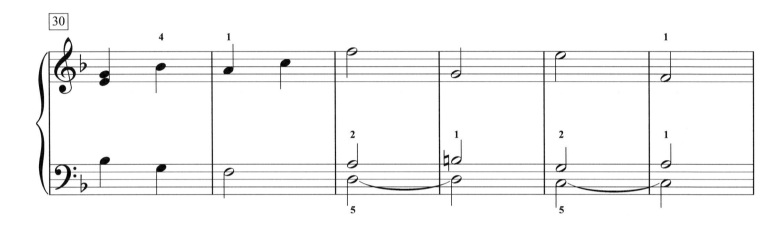

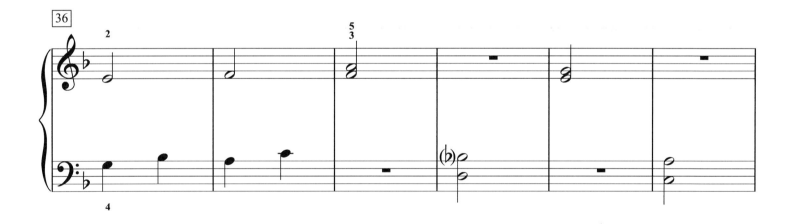

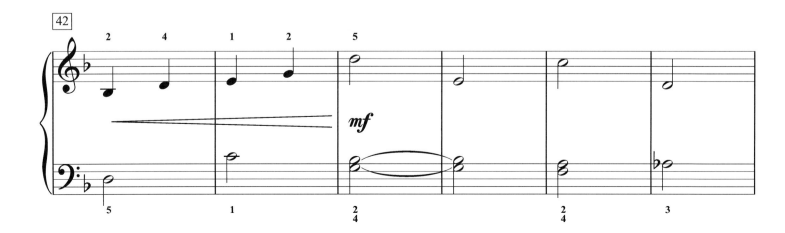

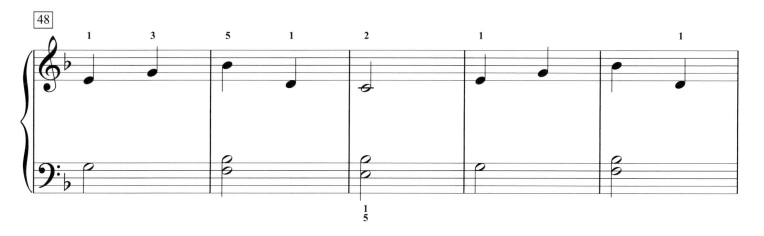

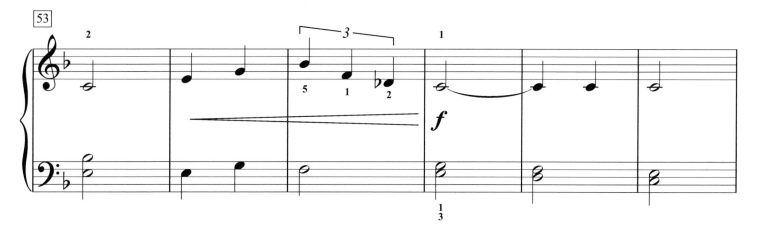

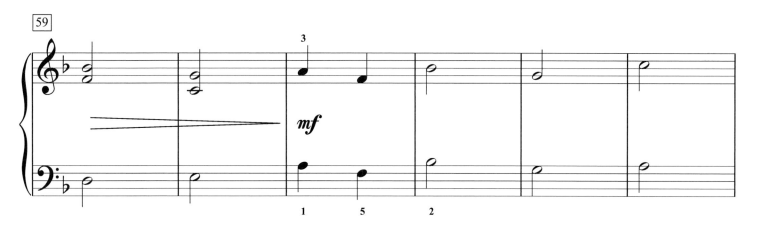

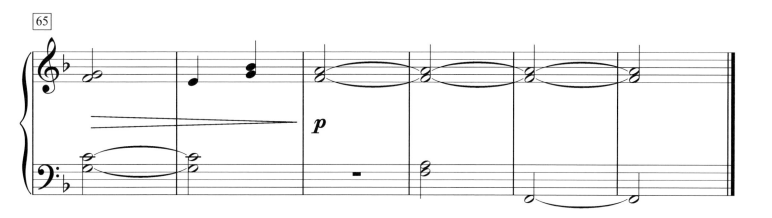

Spring (1st movement)
from THE FOUR SEASONS

Use after Group I (page 4)

Composed by Antonio Vivaldi
Arranged by Christopher Hussey

TRACKS
3–4

Allegro

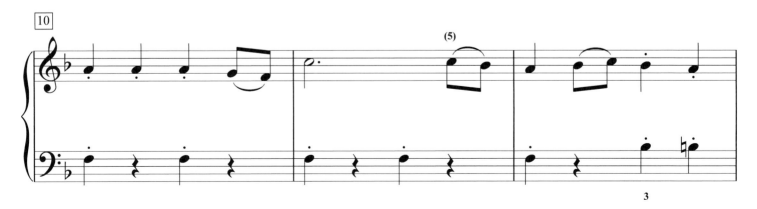

In Tears Of Grief

from ST. MATTHEW PASSION

Use after Group II (page 9)

TRACKS 5–6

Composed by Johann Sebastian Bach
Arranged by Christopher Hussey

Largo

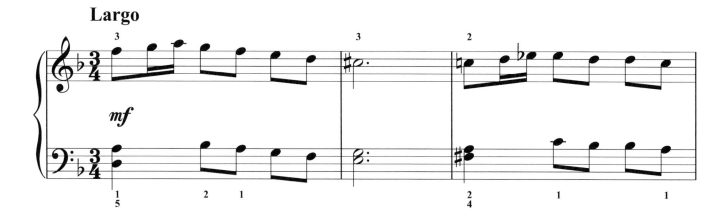

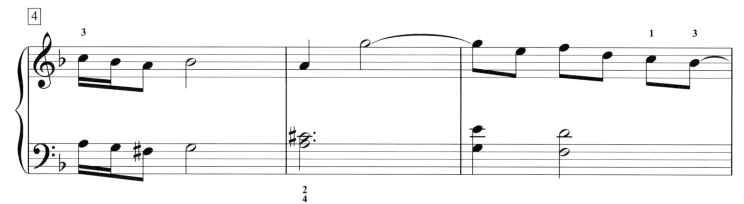

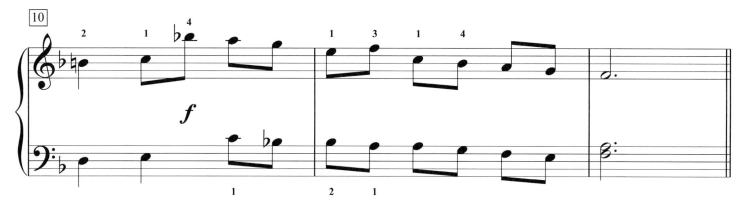

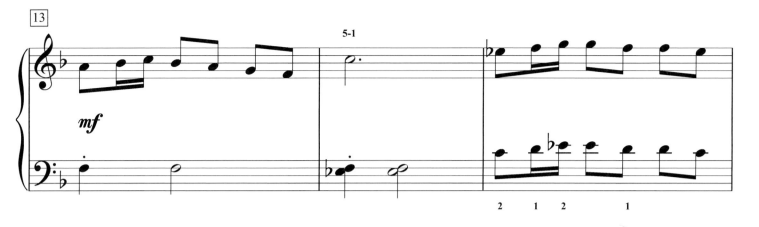

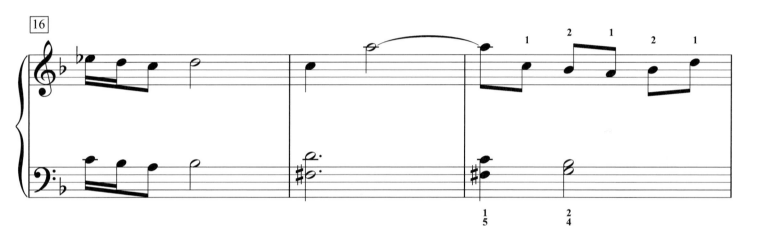

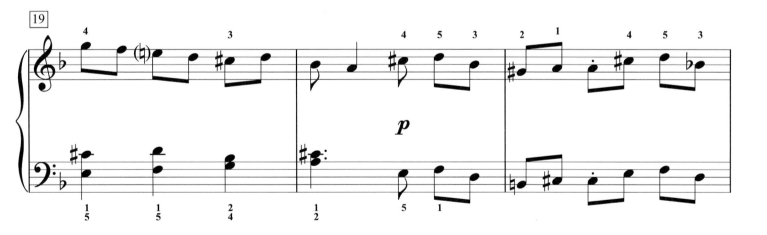

Air
from THE WATER MUSIC
Use after Group II (page 9)

TRACKS
7–8

Composed by George Frideric Handel
Arranged by Christopher Hussey

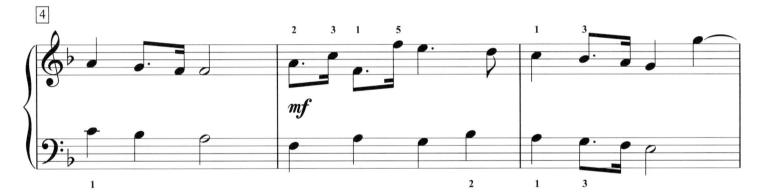

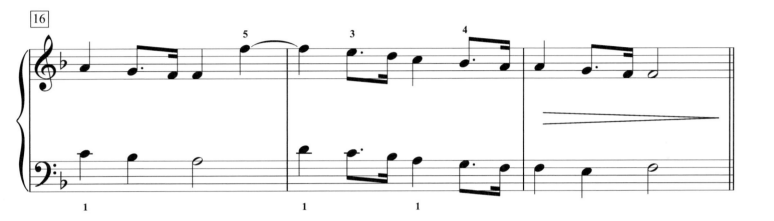

12

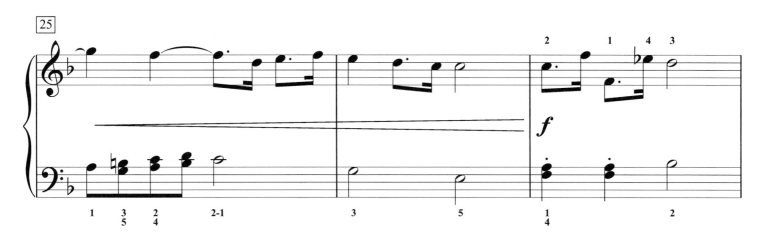

molto rit.

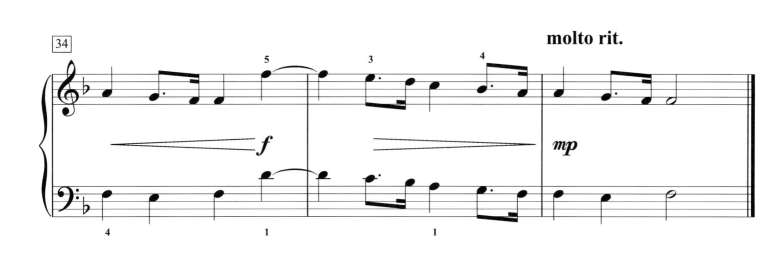

Nocturne from String Quartet No.2

Use after Group III (page 14)

TRACKS 9–10

Composed by Alexander Borodin
Arranged by Christopher Hussey

Andante

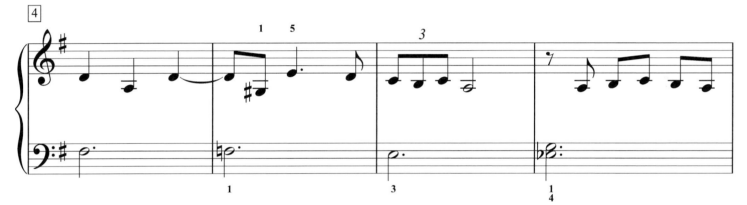

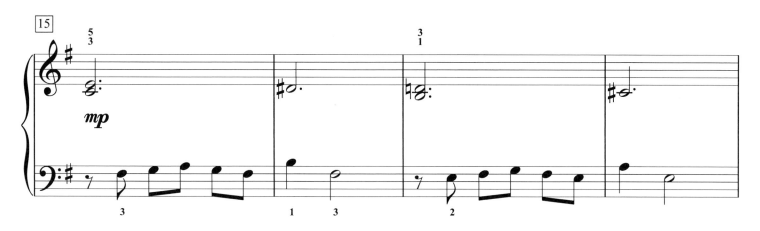

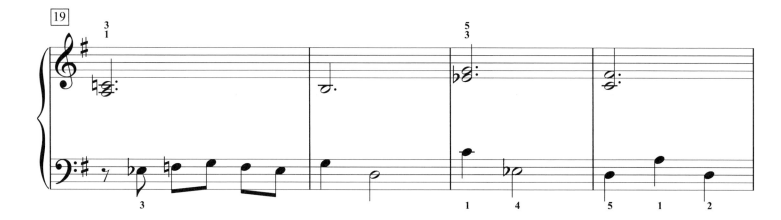

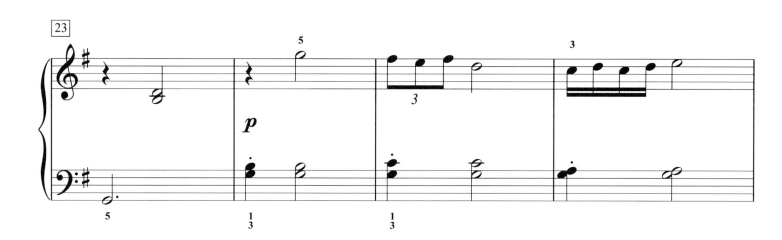

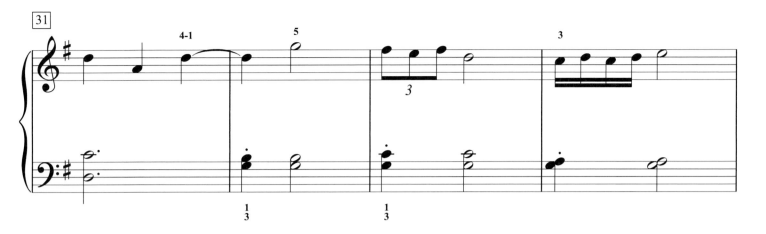

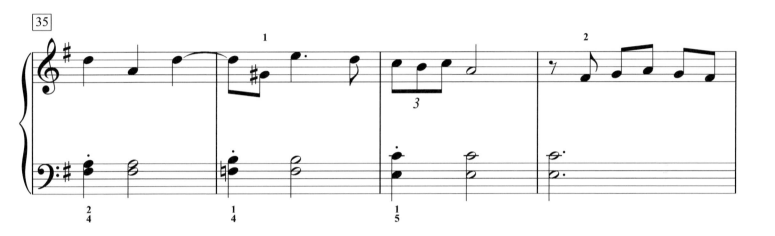

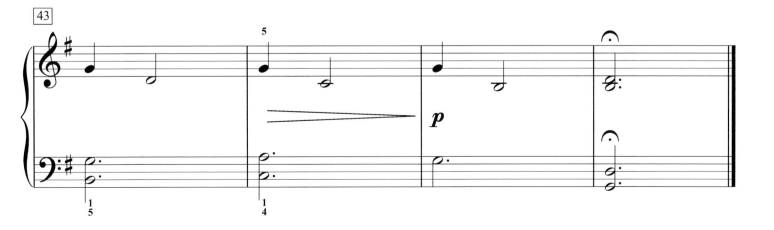

Piano Concerto No.1

2nd movement: Romance

Use after Group III (page 14)

TRACKS
11–12

Composed by Frédéric Chopin
Arranged by Christopher Hussey

Moderato

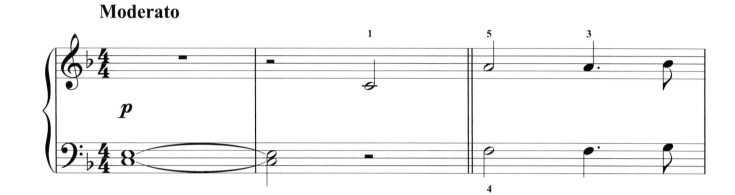

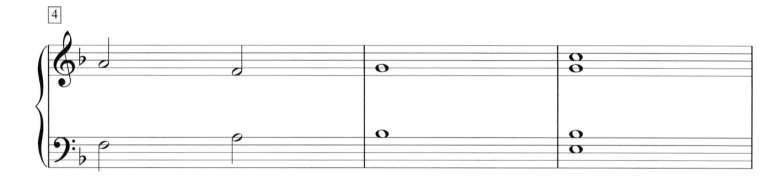

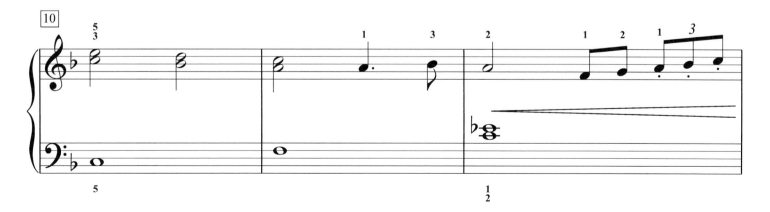

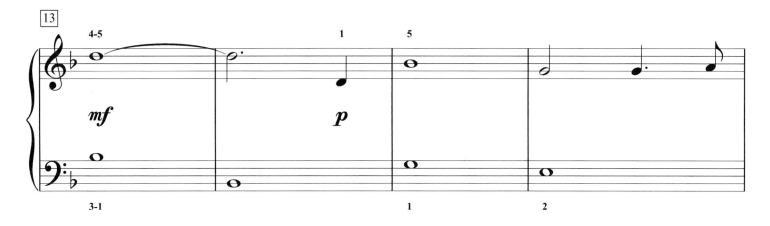

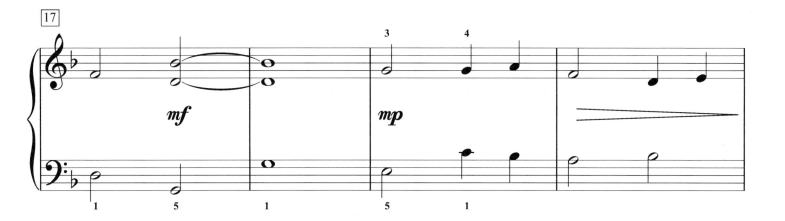

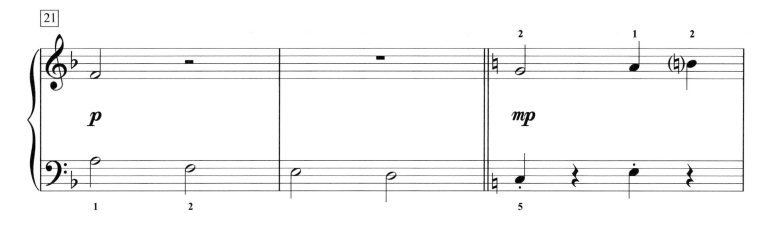

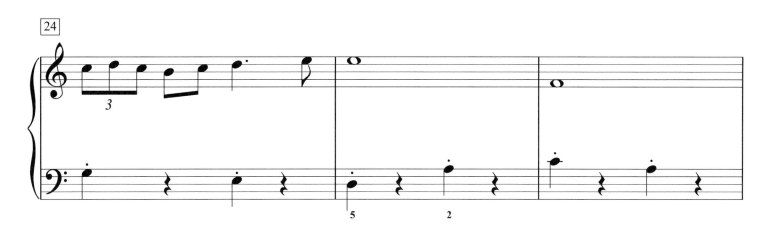

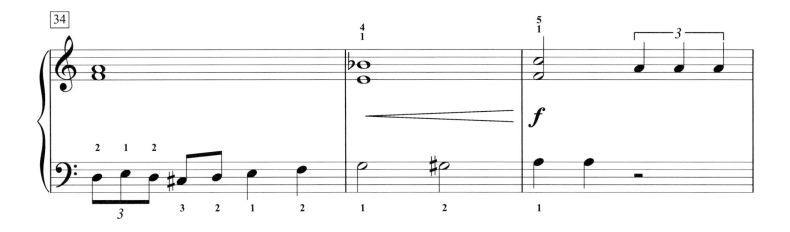

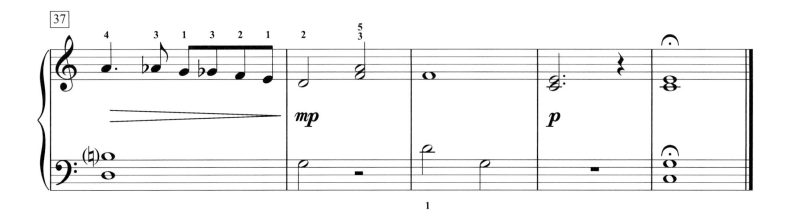

Pavane

Use after Group IV (page 20)

TRACKS
13–14

Composed by Gabriel Fauré
Arranged by Christopher Hussey

Andante

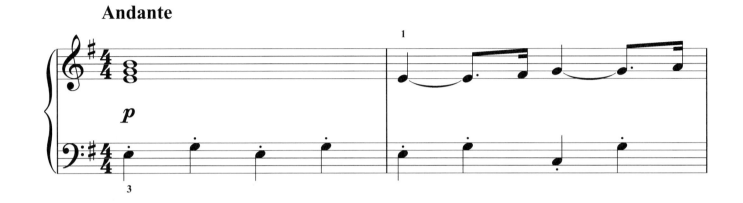

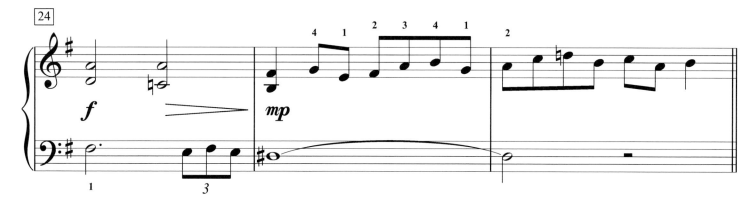

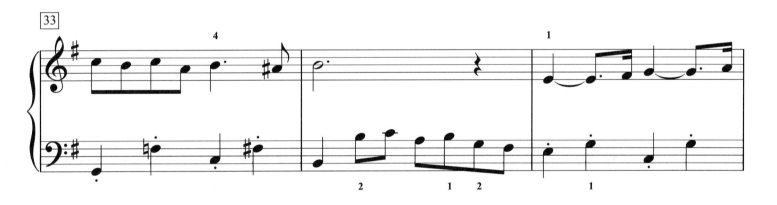

Meditation
from THAÏS

Use after Group IV (page 20)

TRACKS
15–16

Composed Jules Massenet
Arranged by Christopher Hussey

Religioso

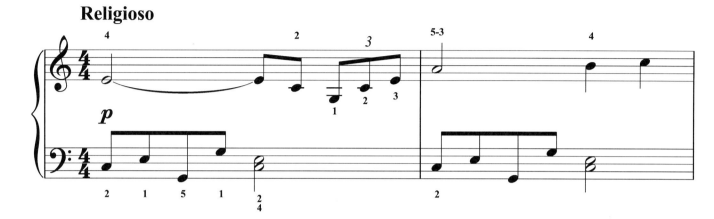

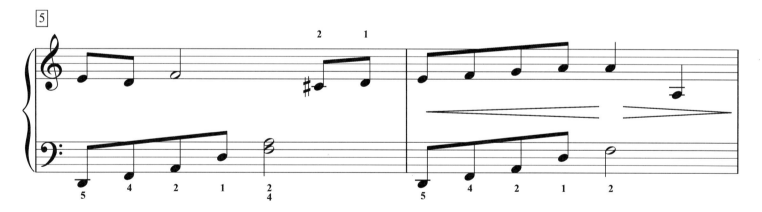

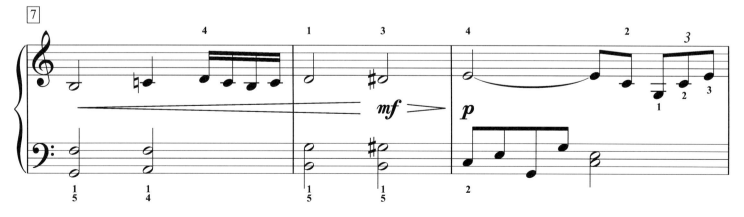

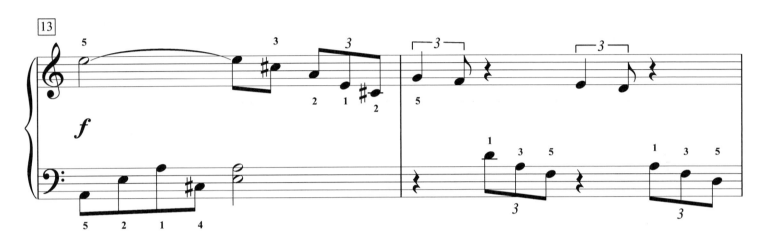

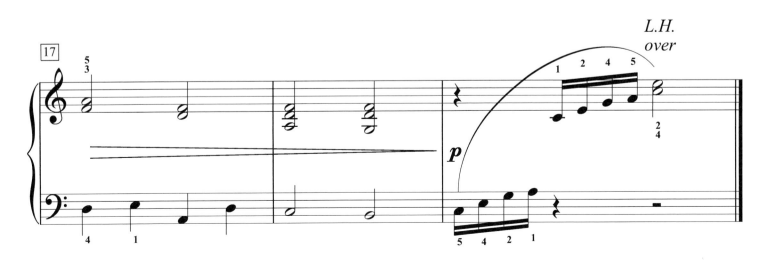

Dance Of The Sugar Plum Fairy

from THE NUTCRACKER

Use after Group V (page 28)

TRACKS
17–18

Composed by Pyotr Ilyich Tchaikovsky
Arranged by Christopher Hussey

Andante non troppo

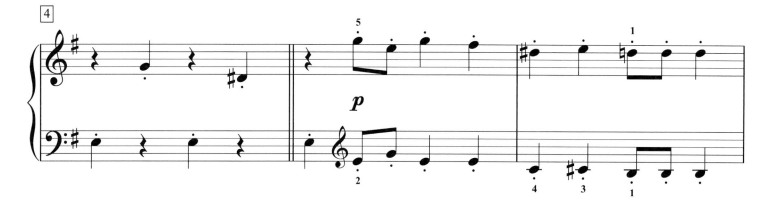

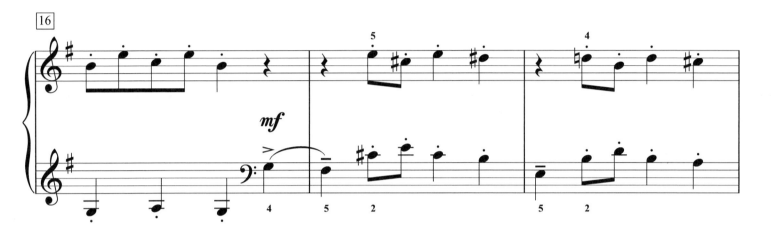

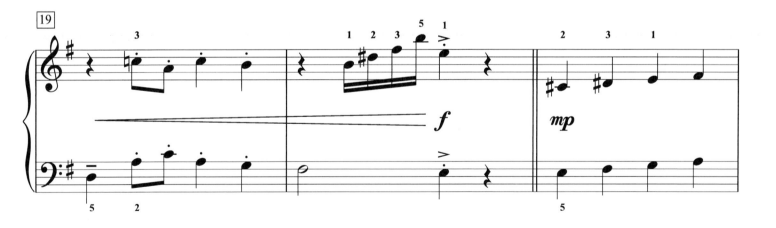

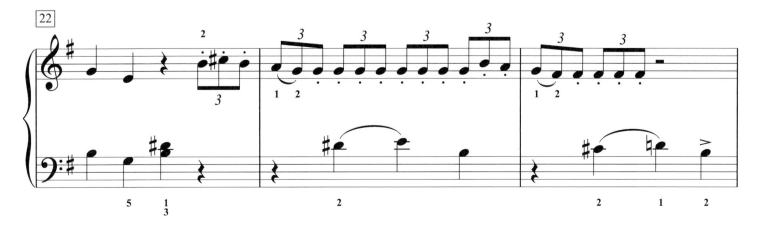

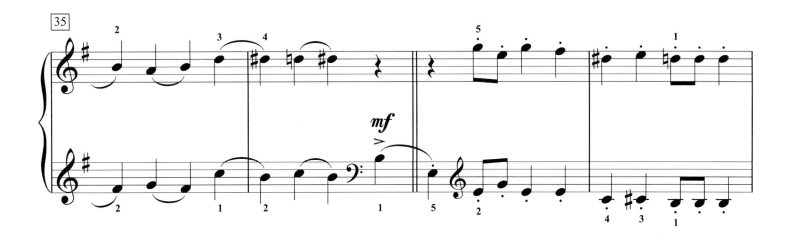

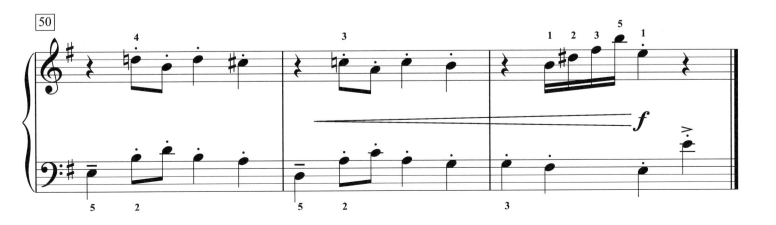

Eine Kleine Nachtmusik, K525

1st movement

Use after Group V (page 28)

TRACKS 19–20

Composed by Wolfgang Amadeus Mozart
Arranged by Christopher Hussey

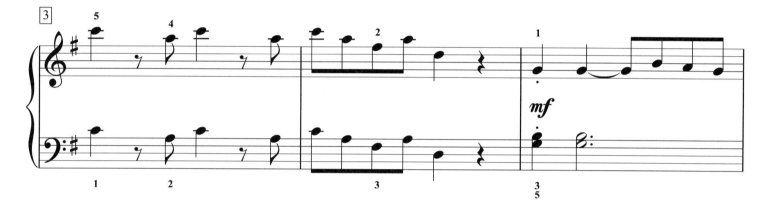

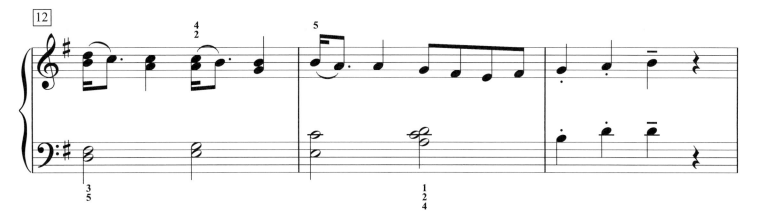

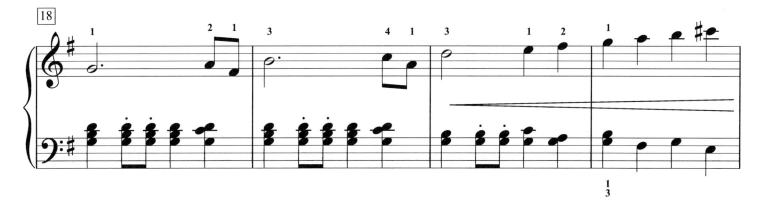

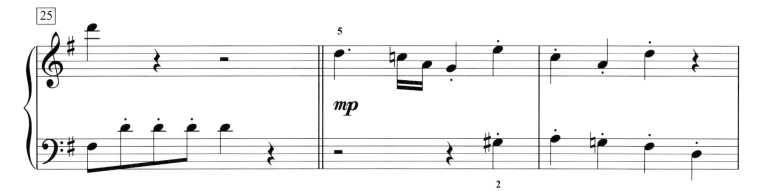

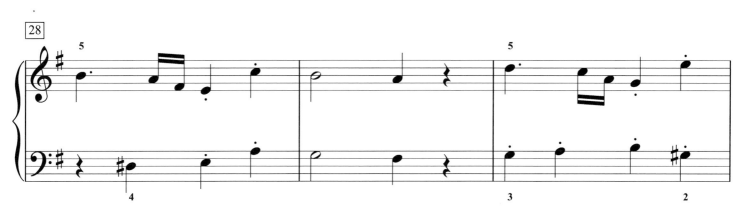

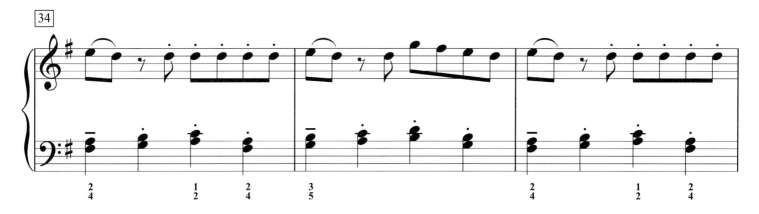

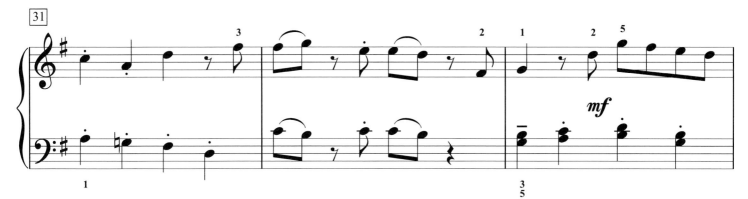

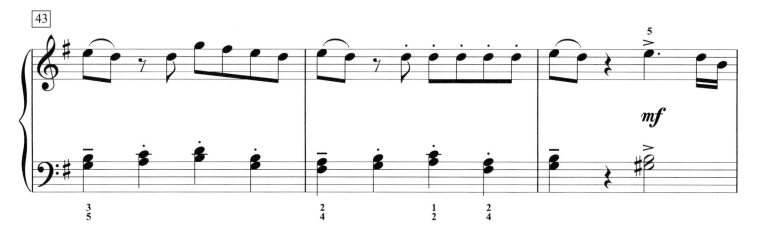

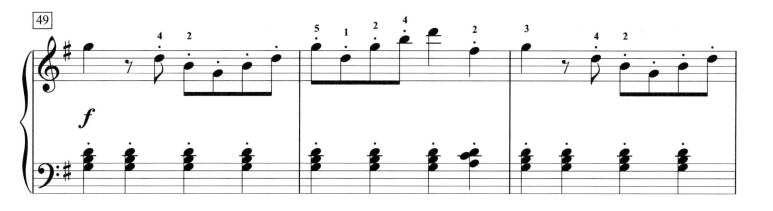